ACTION SPANISH!

What is *Action Spanish!*?

Action Spanish! is designed as a "treasure chest" of activities and games for learning Spanish. Use it as an extra resource in a class or group or at home with your own children. You don't have to be fluent in Spanish–learn along with the children. You can adapt the material for a range of ages, from 3 to 10. Pick and choose from the ideas here to create your own language sessions. Even if you use only one idea and it's successful, that's fine!

Before you start–familiarize yourself with the contents of the *Action Spanish!* pack.

In the book itself you will find:
★ Words and Phrases (pages 2 and 3)
★ Activities and Games (pages 4 to 10)
★ Rhymes and Songs (pages 11 and 12)

In the center of the book you will find a "pullout" section that includes:
★ Treasure Hunt board game
★ Body and Clothes (back of board game)
★ Labels for the house
★ Themed flash cards

On the inside covers of the book are:
★ Supercat mask and finger puppet templates
★ Badges and game counters
★ Instructions on how to use the templates and pull-out pages.

In addition there is:
★ **A recording**–with all the words and phrases, and the rhymes and songs, including "karaoke" versions to sing along to.
★ **A poster**–of weather, days of the week, months of the year, the seasons, numbers, and the alphabet.

Children learning languages

The earlier you start learning a language, the better. Children are curious about new people and places and are not at all inhibited about making strange sounds. They don't worry about making mistakes, and they are proud of their achievements. These are all wonderful language-learning qualities! The trick is to make sure children enjoy the experience of learning. That is the aim of *Action Spanish!*.

★ Keep the Spanish sessions short but as regular as possible.
★ Stimulate all the children's senses, with sounds, colors, shapes, smells, and movement. The book has ideas on this.
★ If you have only one child, invite a friend over to the Spanish sessions. It's more fun to learn in a small group.
★ Take every opportunity to have a genuine "Spanish experience", meeting Spanish speakers or travelling to Mexico, Spain, or another Spanish-speaking country.

This is **Supergato** (Supercat). Look out for him and his worst enemy, **Monstruo-rata** (Monsterat), and family. They speak only Spanish!

¡Hola!

1

Words and Phrases

Here are some basic words and expressions that can be taught using the Activities and Games (pages 4-10). Listen to them on the recording to practice their pronunciation. You can refer to them at any time, so you don't need to learn them all at once! *You will find other important words on the labels, the flash cards, the poster, and the back of the board game. They are also on the recording.*

Saying "Hello"

buenos días	good morning
hola	hello, hi
adiós	good-bye
buenas tardes	good evening
buenas noches	good night
¿cómo te llamas?	what's your name?
me llamo	my name is
¿cuántos años tienes?	how old are you?
tengo…años	I'm…years old
ésta es/éste es…	this is…
¿qué tal?	how are you?
muy bien, gracias	very well, thanks
¡estoy muy mal!	I'm feeling awful!

Family and friends

mamá	mom
papá	dad
mi madre	my mother
mi padre	my father
mi hermana	my sister
mi hermano	my brother
mi abuela	my grandmother
mi abuelo	my grandfather
mi amiga *(girl)*	my friend
mi amigo *(boy)*	my friend
mis amigas *(girls)*	my friends
mis amigos *(boys, mixed)*	my friends

General expressions

sí	yes
no	no
gracias	thank you
por favor	please
aquí/allí	here/there
es	it's
son	these are
hay	there is
voy	I'm going
soy/estoy	I am
tengo	I have
no tengo	I don't have

Shopping and eating

quiero…	I'd like…
esto/esta	this
pequeño/pequeña	little
grande	big
aquí tienes	here you are
tengo hambre	I'm hungry
tengo sed	I'm thirsty
me gusta *(s)*/me gustan *(pl)*	I like
no me gusta *(s)* no me gustan *(pl)*	I don't like
¿cuánto es?	how much is it?
¿ya está?	is that all?

2

Useful instructions

dame	pass me, give me
tráeme	bring me
toma	take (it)
¡de prisa!	quickly!
¿listo/lista?	ready?
me toca a mí	my turn
te toca a ti	your turn
¡he ganado!	I've won!
¡bravo!	well done!
muy bien	very good
estupendo	great
¡vamos!	let's go!
¡voy!	I'm coming!
¡que duermas bien!	sleep well!
¡que aproveche!	enjoy your meal!

Pastimes

leo	I read (or I'm reading)
veo la televisión	I watch TV
escucho música	I listen to music
canto	I sing
bailo	I dance
juego	I play
juego al fútbol	I play soccer
¡no hago nada!	I don't do anything!
me gusta leer	I like reading
me gusta ver la tele	I like watching TV
me gusta escuchar música	I like listening to music
me gusta cantar	I like singing
me gusta bailar	I like dancing
me gusta jugar	I like playing
me gusta jugar al fútbol	I like playing soccer

Useful questions

¿qué es esto?	what is it/this?
¿de qué color es?	what color is it?
¿quién es?	who is it?
¿quieres?	would you like?
¿qué quieres?	what would you like?
¿qué haces?	what are you doing?
¿te gusta/te gustan?	do you like?
¿te gusta leer/cantar?	do you like reading/singing?
¿qué te gusta hacer?	what do you like doing?
¿qué quieres hacer?	what do you want to do?
¿dónde está?	where is?
¿dónde están?	where are?

Telling the time

¿qué hora es?	what's the time?
son las dos	it's two o'clock
son las tres y media	it's half past three
son las cuatro y cuarto	it's a quarter after four
son las cinco menos cuarto	it's a quarter to five
es mediodía	it's noon
es medianoche	it's midnight

Activities and Games

Spanish once a day...

Every day may be a bit ambitious, though it's ideal if you can manage it. Try to build some simple Spanish into your routine:

★ Pin up the poster in a prominent place. Mark the days of the week with a paper clip. Note the weather each day.
★ Learn a few basic phrases such as "pass me" or "thank you" or "let's go" or "I'm coming" (see pages 2 and 3). Use them regularly, or at a set time, like breakfast, lunch on Saturday, or on the way to school.
★ Count things, such as your footsteps, or while you kick a ball or set the table.
★ Buy some simple Spanish picture books or cassettes and have a cuddly bedtime story. Make it a special treat.
★ Play the recording in the car and sing along with the songs.

Spanish corner

Create a Spanish corner in your house or classroom.

★ Collect Spanish things to put in the corner, such as stamps, Spanish books, Mexican food, menus and bills.
★ Draw and color a poster of the Spanish flag to decorate the corner. If you have Spanish pen pals (see page 10), you can keep their letters and photos in the corner. If it's a large corner, you could hold your Spanish sessions there!

New Spanish words

Before you start a game, spend a few minutes introducing the new words and phrases–but not too many at a time. (They are on the recording.)

Note that in Spanish "**el**" and "**la**" mean "the" while "**un**" and "**una**" mean "a."
For example:
el gato (the cat), **un gato** (a cat); or
la boca (the mouth), **una boca** (a mouth).

★ Listen and repeat the words. Clap to help pronunciation, especially the syllables of longer words.
★ Use the flash cards. Point to the number or picture and say its name clearly. Gesture for the children to repeat it.
★ Hold up cards randomly and ask questions that the children can answer **Sí** (Yes) or **No** (No). For example: **¿Es...azul?** (Is it...blue?).
★ Turn the cards face down. The children can pick one out and say the word, or ask the question **¿Qué es esto?** (What is it?).

4

Label your house

Cut out the labels from the center pages. Use a removable adhesive to attach them so they can easily be moved around.

★ Stick up different ones each day or each week. If you leave them too long, they will lose their impact.
★ Make it into a game. Hold the labels out in a fan, face down like a pack of cards, and ask the children to pick one. They can say the word out loud or repeat it after you, and then go and stick it in the right place.

★ Stick some around the house and ask a question, e.g. : **¿Dónde está la tele?** (Where is the TV?). The children can show you.
★ To collect the labels, say, for example, **Tráeme la taza** (Bring me the cup).
★ Make your own labels, too. See Spanish Arts and Crafts (page 9) for ideas.

Tráeme...

Pairs game

For 2 or more players

This familiar game is especially useful for practicing the words on the flash cards.

★ Shuffle the cards and lay them all out face down.
★ Take turns. Turn over two cards and say the Spanish words out loud.
★ If they are a pair, say **Sí** (Yes) or **Sí, tengo una pareja** (Yes, I have a pair), and keep them. If not, turn them back over in exactly the same position and say **No** (No) or **No, no tengo una pareja** (No, I don't have a pair).
★ The player with the most pairs wins.

With very young children, use only three pairs to start with and work up to more. Older children could try guessing the card before they turn it over. Use either one word, like **¿Azul?** (Blue?) or **¿Queso?** (Cheese?), or a simple phrase like **¿Es el azul?** (Is it the blue?) or **¿Es el queso?** (Is it the cheese?)

Activities and Games

cinco

Lotto

For 2 players

Another fun way to practice flash card words.

★ Put one card from each flash card pair into a bag or box.
★ Deal out the remaining cards to the players.
★ Pick a card from the bag and say the word out loud in Spanish.
★ The player who has its pair says **Sí** (Yes) or **Sí, tengo…el cinco** (Yes, I have…the five). Give that player the card. Other players say **No** (No) or **No, no tengo una pareja** (No, I don't have a pair).
★ The first player to have all pairs calls out **¡He ganado!** (I've won!)

Sí, tengo el cinco

Packing a suitcase

This popular travel game is a lively way to practice the Spanish words for clothes. (See the back of the board game.)

★ Take turns saying **Hago mi maleta y pongo…** (I'm packing my suitcase and I put in…) and then choosing something to put in the suitcase–for example, **un sombrero** (a hat).
★ Each person *repeats* the list and adds another thing, so: **Hago mi maleta y pongo un sombrero…y un vestido** (I'm packing my suitcase and I put in a hat… and a dress).
★ You might run out of memory before you run out of words!

Let's go shopping

This is a similar game to the packing one above, but instead you go shopping.

★ Take turns saying **Voy a la tienda y voy a comprar…** (I'm going to the store and I'm going to buy…), then each player adds one thing, like **un tomate** (a tomato).

You can adapt this game to practice any themed vocabulary–seeing farm animals, for example: **Estoy en la granja y veo…** (I'm at the farm and I see…).

dining room	kitchen	living room
door	stairs	hall
rug, carpet	mirror	radiator
lamp	table	chair
basin	shower	bath
refrigerator	oven	stove
spoon	knife	fork
radio	video recorder	TV
pencil	ballpoint pen	fountain pen
eyeglasses	toys	bicycle

la sala de estar	la cocina	el comedo
el vestíbulo	la escalera	la puerta
el radiador	el espejo	la alfombr
la silla	la mesa	la lámpara
el baño	la ducha	el lavabo
la estufa	el horno	el refrigerado
el tenedor	el cuchillo	la cuchara
la tele	la videocasetera	la radio
la pluma	el bolígrafo	el lápiz
la bicicleta	los juguetes	las gafas

el helado	el pan	el chocolate	el queso
el tomate	la leche	la manzana	el agua
el pastel	el plátano	la mermelada	el jamón
la cola	los espaguetis	el sándwich	la pizza

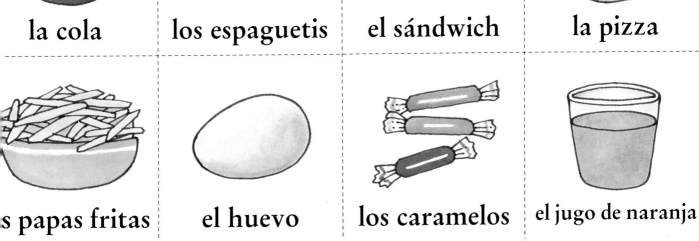

s papas fritas	el huevo	los caramelos	el jugo de naranja

1 uno	2 dos	3 tres	4 cuatro
5 cinco	6 seis	7 siete	8 ocho
9 nueve	10 diez	11 once	12 doce
13 trece	14 catorce	15 quince	16 dieciséis
17 diecisiete	18 dieciocho	19 diecinueve	20 veinte

rojo, roja	azul	amarillo, amarilla	verde
naranja	negro, negra	blanco, blanca	morado, morada
rosa	gris	marrón	0 cero
el perro	el gato	el conejo	el caballo
el ratón	el pato	la oveja	la vaca

La ropa
(clothes)

Fill in the spaces from the
list of Spanish words below.

----

el abrigo (coat)
el traje de baño (swimsuit)
las botas (boots)
la bufanda (scarf)

los calcetines (socks)
la camiseta (T-shirt)
la falda (skirt)
la gorra (cap)

los guantes (gloves)
los pantalones (pants/trousers)
los pantalones cortos (shorts)
el sombrero (hat)

el suéter (sweater)
el vestido (dress)
las zapatillas (slippers)
los zapatos (shoes)

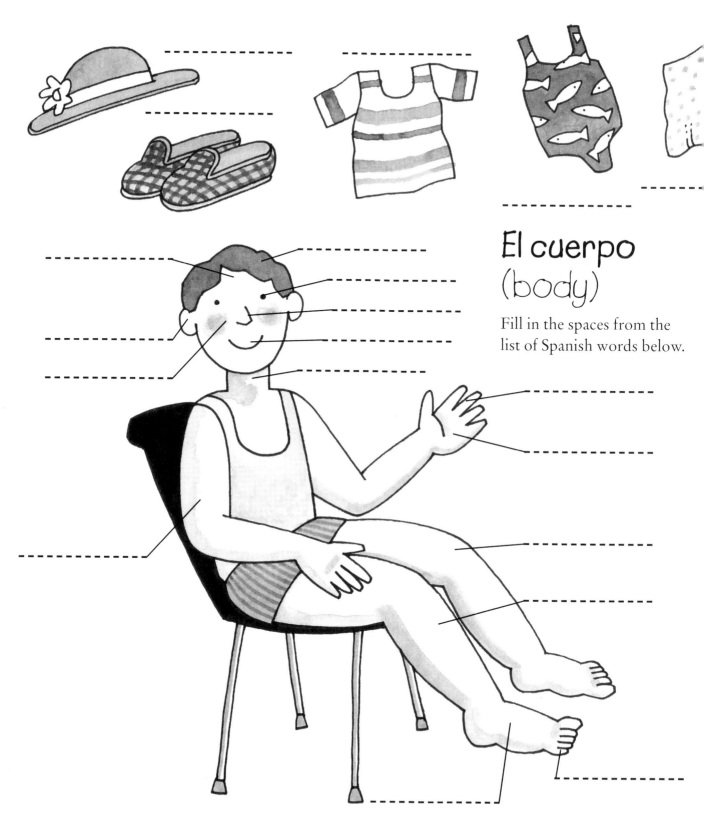

El cuerpo (body)

Fill in the spaces from the list of Spanish words below.

la boca (mouth)
el brazo (arm)
la cabeza (head)
la cara (face)

el cuello (neck)
los dedos (fingers)
los dedos del pie (toes)
la mano (hand)

la nariz (nose)
el ojo (eye)
la oreja (ear)
el pelo (hair)

el pie (foot)
la pierna (leg)
la rodilla (knee)

rojo, roja

azul

amarillo, amarilla

verde

naranja

negro, negra

blanco, blanca

morado, morad

rosa

gris

marrón

0
cero

el perro

el gato

el conejo

el caballo

el ratón

el pato

la oveja

la vaca

1 uno	2 dos	3 tres	4 cuatro
5 cinco	6 seis	7 siete	8 ocho
9 nueve	10 diez	11 once	12 doce
13 trece	14 catorce	15 quince	16 dieciséis
17 diecisiete	18 dieciocho	19 diecinueve	20 veinte

el helado · el pan · el chocolate · el queso

el tomate · la leche · la manzana · el agua

el pastel · el plátano · la mermelada · el jamón

la cola · los espaguetis · el sándwich · la pizza

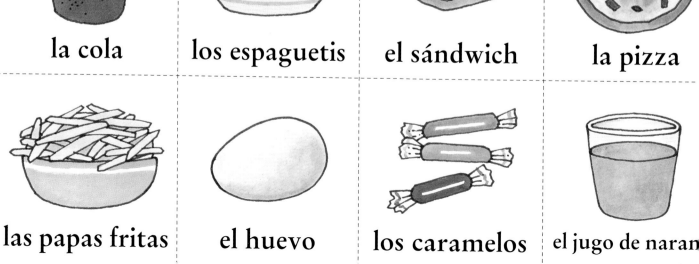

las papas fritas · el huevo · los caramelos · el jugo de naran

dormitorio	el cuarto de baño	el servicio
a ventana	la pared	el techo
la cama	el armario	el sillón
el jarrón	la planta	la aspiradora
el grifo	el cepillo de dientes	la toalla
el tirador de la puerta	el cajón	el cubo de basura
el plato	el vaso	la taza
el teléfono	la computadora	la impresora
la regla	la goma	el libro
la llave	el reloj	el despertador

toilet	bathroom	bedroom
ceiling	wall	window
armchair	wardrobe/cupboard	bed
vacuum cleaner	plant	vase
towel	toothbrush	faucet/tap
trash can/dustbin	drawer	door handle
cup	glass	plate
printer	computer	telephone
book	eraser	ruler
alarm clock	clock/watch	key

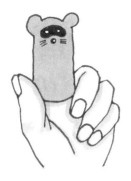

Finger puppets

Make the finger puppets on the inside front cover. They are wonderful for practicing saying "hello" and short conversations.

★ Name the puppets and change your voice so they can "talk" to each other.
★ Hide a puppet and ask **¿Dónde está… Jorge?** (Where is…George?). Answer **¡Aquí!** (Here!) or **¡Estoy aquí!** (I'm here!)
★ Practice other language, like greetings, introducing family and friends, saying name and age, or please and thank you (see also pages 2 and 3). Keep the conversations short and simple. Add new language in stages.

Supercat mask

Make the mask on the inside front cover.

★ Whoever wears the mask is "Supergato"– who speaks only Spanish!
★ Make sure it's a real treat to wear the mask. That person can wear the **Hablo español** (I speak Spanish) badge too.
★ Build up the "mask language" slowly. At first, whoever wears the mask could just say **¡Hola!** (Hi!). Then the child could say **Me llamo…** (My name is…) or **Me llamo Supergato** (My name is Supercat) and their age: **Tengo ocho años** (I'm eight), and perhaps **Hablo español** (I speak Spanish). Players can progress to saying what their likes and dislikes are, what they enjoy doing, and what day it is, and asking questions.
★ Whoever wears the mask could win a bonus, such as starting first in the games.
★ Use the mask as a reward for winning a game.

Guess what?

Use this game to practice new words.

★ Put some small objects on a tray: an apple, a key, a pencil, a fork, a candy. (If necessary learn some new words.) Cover the tray with a cloth.
★ Uncover the tray and allow the children a short time to look at the objects.
★ Then quickly cover the tray again.
★ Players have to try to remember the objects and say them out loud in Spanish.
★ Try using the phrase **Hay…** (There is…).
★ For a variation, put the objects in a bag and guess what it contains by feeling.

Activities and Games

Ugh!

Use this game to practice saying **Me gusta** (I like) and **No me gusta** (I don't like).

★ Collect bottles or yogurt containers and fill them with various smells, like rose petals, banana, mint, coffee beans, soap.
★ Fill other containers with things to touch–peeled grapes, a damp sponge, sand, a leaf.
★ Smell or touch something and say **Me gusta esto** (I like this) or **No me gusta esto** (I don't like this). Make appropriate faces and gestures!
★ Then let the children sniff or feel and tell you what they think. It is more exciting if they are lightly blindfolded.

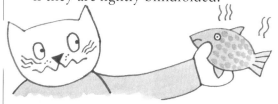

Charades

Adapt this game to practice saying what you *like* doing, e.g. **Me gusta leer** (I like reading). Review the phrases on page 3 before you start.

★ One person mimes a favorite activity. The others have to guess. They can ask a question such as **¿Te gusta leer?** (Do you like reading?), or give an answer: **Te gusta leer** (You like reading). The person miming answers either **No** (No) if it's the wrong guess, or **Sí, me gusta leer** (Yes, I like reading), if the guess is right.
★ To practice saying what you are doing now, one person mimes. The others ask **¿Qué haces?** (What are you doing?), and the actor gives the answer, for example **Leo** (I'm reading).

Let's pretend

Use role play and little dramas to practice "real-life" situations, particularly shopping or introducing friends or family. Dress up and use simple homemade props to set the scenes.

★ Review the phrases beforehand–this can be the show rehearsal.
★ For older children write prompt notes on cards. For example: "You are a storekeeper. Say hello. Ask, How are you?" or "You are the customer. Ask for some cheese."
★ It's fun to use Spanish names and, as they do in Spain and Latin America, **señor**, **señora**, and **señorita**, without a surname.
★ Keep it short and simple.
★ Below are two role-play examples. Rather than simply reading them aloud, use them as a guide and let the children improvise.

These two conversations are recorded.

Shopping

Storekeeper	**Buenos días.**
Customer	**Buenos días. Quiero...tres manzanas y dos plátanos, por favor.**
Storekeeper	**Aquí tienes. ¿Ya está?**
Customer	**Sí, ¿cuánto es?**
Storekeeper	**Cien.**
Customer	**Gracias.**
Storekeeper	**Adiós.**

Saying "hello" to family and friends

1st person (Jaime)	**¡Hola, Juan!**
2nd person (Juan)	**¡Hola, Jaime! ¿Qué tal?**
1st person (Jaime)	**Bien, gracias. Éste es mi padre.**
2nd person (Juan)	**Buenos días, señor.**
3rd person (el padre)	**Buenos días, Juan.**
1st person (Jaime)	**Y ésta es mi hermana, María.**
2nd person (Juan)	**¡Hola, María!**
4th person (María)	**¡Hola, Juan!**

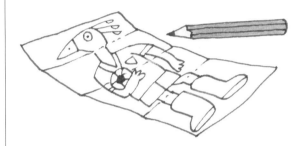

Heads, bodies, and legs

Review the parts of the body first (see the back of the board game).

★ Each player has a blank piece of paper.
★ Give instructions in stages:
  Dibuja la cabeza (Draw the head), then
  Dibuja el cuerpo (Draw the body), then
  Dibuja las piernas (Draw the legs), and
  finally **Dibuja los pies** (Draw the feet).
★ After each stage, players fold the paper over to hide their drawing (leaving a tiny bit showing) and pass it to their neighbor to add on the next stage.
★ The children could chant as they draw **Dibujo la cabeza** (I'm drawing the head), etc.
★ Once they're confident, the children can give the instructions. Older children could label each stage.

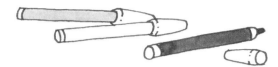

Spanish arts and crafts

Apply art and design skills to learning Spanish!

★ Make extra flash cards or room labels with the children. Cut pictures out of magazines, stick them on cardboard and label them.
★ Make badges with special messages.
★ Make birthday cards, Christmas cards, and cards for other special occasions. Here are some useful phrases:
  Feliz cumpleaños (Happy birthday)
  Feliz Navidad (Merry Christmas)
  Próspero Año Nuevo (Happy New Year)
  Felices Pascuas (Happy Easter)
  Saludos de… (Hello from…)
★ Draw self-portraits and use them to learn the parts of the body and clothes. (See the back of the board game.) Younger children can answer the question **¿Qué es?** (What's that?) with the answers **Es la cabeza** (It's the head) or **Es un zapato** (It's a shoe). Older children can label them too.

¡Feliz cumpleaños!

Activities and Games

Active Spanish

Young children won't want to sit still for a long time. Here are some ideas to get them moving but still speaking Spanish.

★ Count while skipping or bouncing balls.
★ Play a version of musical chairs using the flash cards. Put one chair for each child in a row, and one card (e.g. numbers) on each chair. While the music plays, the children walk around the chairs. When the music stops, call out one number. The children may sit down on any chair except the one with that number. The person without a chair is out. Take one chair away each time.
★ Use the songs on page 12 to dance and sing along to the tunes. Make up actions too.
★ Play **¿Qué hora es, señor Lobo?** (What's the time, Mr. Wolf?) to practice telling the time with older children. Stick to simple times at first. The wolf, **señor Lobo**, walks around the room and everyone follows, taking turns to call out **¿Qué hora es, señor Lobo?** The wolf answers a time; for example: **Son las dos** (It's two o'clock) or **Son las diez** (It's ten o'clock). But if he answers **¡Es la hora de comer!** (It's lunch time!), they all must try to escape when he chases them! Whoever is caught plays **señor Lobo** next.
★ You can adapt this to practice weather: **¿Qué tiempo hace, señor Lobo?** (What's the weather like, Mr. Wolf?). Escape if he says **Llueve!** (It's raining!)
★ You could also rename the wolf "Supergato" and he can wear the mask.

Pen pals

A direct link with a friend in Mexico, or another Spanish-speaking country gives language learning a purpose and shows that there are *real* people who *always* speak Spanish!

★ You can write in English with some simple phrases in Spanish. Exchange photos, postcards, and small objects from your daily life. If your pen pal writes in Spanish, learn the useful phrases.
★ If you are with a day-care center, club, or school, you can pair up with a similar organization and send group messages.
★ Exchange audio cassettes. Children can hear their friends' voices and build up their stocks of Spanish songs and rhymes.
★ Using E-mail is much faster. If you have the right equipment, you can even send pictures and voice messages.
★ Here are a few phrases to start you off:
  Querido (Dear, *to a boy*)
  Querida (Dear, *to a girl*),
  Gracias por tu carta (Thank you for your letter)
  ¡Escribe pronto! (Write soon!)
  Un abrazo (Best wishes, a hug)

See also the book *Pen Pals* from Passport Books.

Rhymes and Songs

Tengo, tengo, tengo

Tengo, tengo, tengo
Tú no tienes nada.
Tengo tres ovejas
En una cabaña.
Una me da leche,
Otra me da lana,
Otra me da queso
Toda la semana.

tengo = I've got
tú no tienes nada = you've got nothing
en una cabaña = in a shack
una me da = one gives me
otra me da = another gives me
lana = wool
toda la semana = all through the week

ACTIONS
• *shake one finger for "nothing"*
• *hold up three fingers for sheep*
• *make both hands into a shack (like a tent)*
• *count off three fingers*
• *at the end, open both hands wide*

El juego chirimbolo

El juego chirimbolo
¡Qué bonito es!
Un pie, otro pie
Una mano, otra mano
Un codo, otro codo

el juego = the game
chirimbolo = thingamajig
¡qué bonito es! = it's such fun!
otro = the other
un codo = one elbow

ACTIONS
• *put out foot, then hand, then elbow*
• *repeat with other parts of the body
  (see back of board game)*

Al corro la patata

Al corro la patata
Comeremos ensalada
Lo que comen los señores
Naranjitas y limones
Alupé, alupé
Sentadita me quedé

al corro la patata = "ring around the" potato
comeremos ensalada = we'll eat salad
lo que comen los señores = what the grown-ups eat
naranjitas y limones = little oranges and lemons
sentadita me quedé = I'll stay sitting down

ACTIONS
*This is like "Ring around the rosies". Hold hands in
a circle and dance round chanting, until you get to
"Alupé, alupé," when you all fall down! Stay sitting
for the last line.*

Songs

Los animales (animals)

¿Dónde está el gato gris?
Gato gris, gato gris
¿Dónde está el gato gris?
      ¿Y el ratón?

Un gato, dos perros, tres patos,
      ¿dónde están?
Un gato, dos perros,
      y un gran ratón.

Songs

Un helado (an ice cream)

Un helado, por favor.
¡Hace mucho calor!
Una cola, por favor.
¡Hace mucho calor!

Sí...sí me gusta.
Tengo hambre, tengo sed.
Sí, sí me gusta.
Gracias, ¿cuánto es?

Un helado, por favor.
¡Hace mucho calor!
Una cola, por favor.
¡Siempre mucho calor!
¡Siempre mucho calor!

Los colores (colors)

Azul, amarillo, y marrón y gris
Hay rojo, sí
Y me gusta, sí.

Blanco, morado, y verde y gris
Hay negro y blanco sí, sí.

¿Qué es esto? (what's this?)

¿Qué es esto?
Es un vaso.
Toma el vaso aquí, mamá

¿Qué es esto?
Es un plato.
Toma el plato aquí, papá.

Los números (numbers)

Uno y dos y tres
    Por favor
Uno y dos y tres

Cuatro y cinco y seis
    Por favor
Cuatro y cinco y seis

Siete, ocho, nueve, diez
    Ocho, nueve, diez

Uno y dos y tres
    Por favor
Uno y dos y tres

¡Hola! (hi!)

¡Hola, buenos días!
¿Qué tal, amigas mías?
Gracias, estamos bien, muy bien.

¡Hola, buenos días!
¿Qué tal, amigas mías?
Muy bien, gracias, adiós.